MIND-STRETCHING MATH RIDDLES

THE GRAPES OF MATH

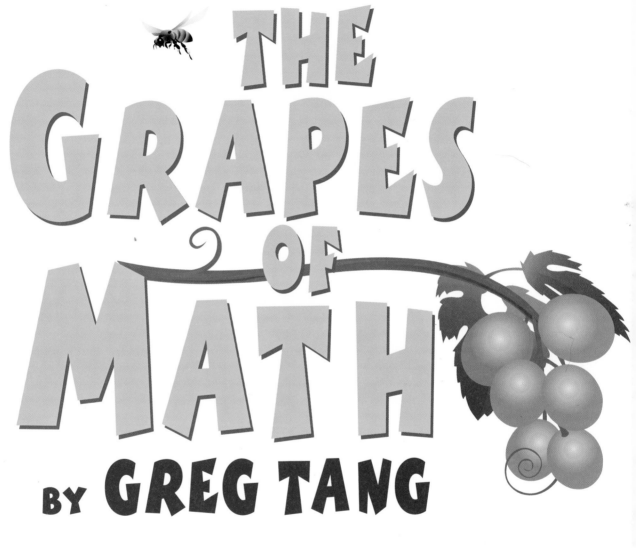

BY GREG TANG

ILLUSTRATED BY
HARRY BRIGGS

SCHOLASTIC INC.

New York Toronto London Auckland Sydney
Mexico City New Delhi Hong Kong Buenos Aires

WITH LOVE TO GREGORY,
EMILY, AND
KATIE

— G.T.

TO KAY EKELIN,
MY GRANDMOTHER

— H.B.

A NOTE ABOUT <u>THE GRAPES OF MATH</u>

Are some kids naturally "good in math"? Or have they learned to think about numbers and problems in more effective ways? *The Grapes of Math* introduces children to the art of problem solving through a series of engaging math riddles. These riddles challenge kids (and parents!) to think creatively while teaching valuable tricks for adding more quickly and accurately.

The Grapes of Math teaches four important lessons in problem solving. The first is to be open-minded. Children will learn to look beyond the obvious in search of smarter solutions. Second, they are encouraged to think strategically by finding convenient sums that make adding easier. Third, kids are taught to save time by using a variety of skills when solving problems, such as subtracting to add. Finally, children learn to organize information by identifying patterns and symmetries.

I hope everybody who reads *The Grapes of Math* enjoys this exciting new approach to problem solving that encourages creativity and common sense, not memorization and formulas. With a little guidance and success, *all* kids can develop the confidence and skills to become good math students and effective problem solvers. Enjoy!

Greg Tang

www.gregtang.com

FIND THE ANSWERS AT THE END OF THE BOOK!

FISH SCHOOL

Of all the creatures in the sea,

A fish is smart as smart can be.

While others swim and play it cool,

A fish is happy in a school!

How many fish are in this class?

Answer quick and you will pass.

Here's a hint, a little clue,

When counting fish, just look askew!

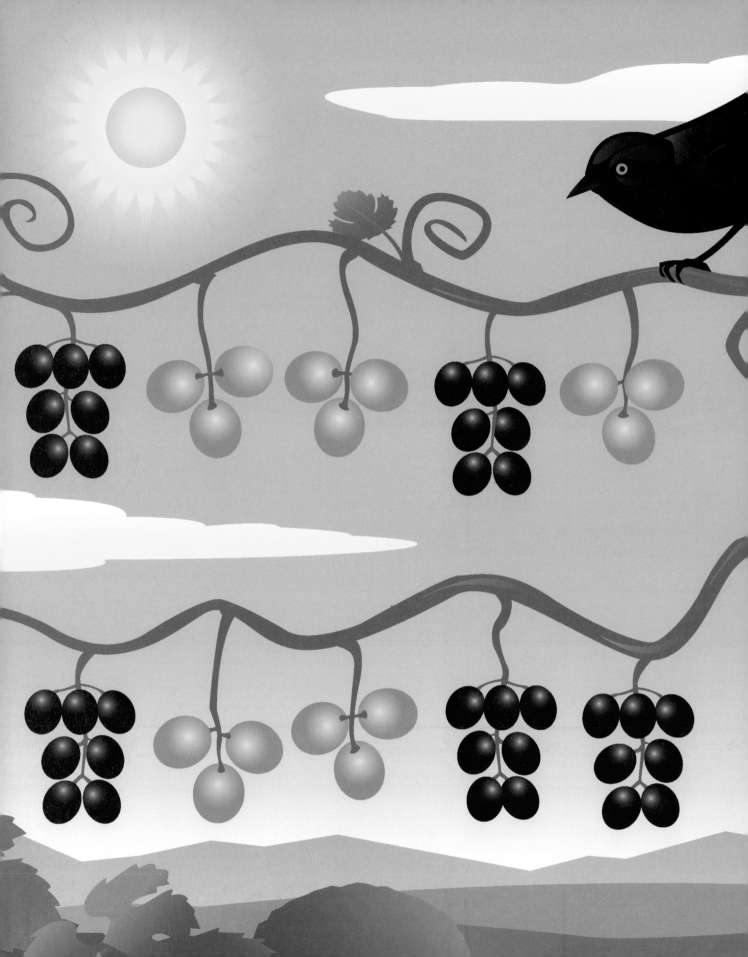

THE GRAPES OF MATH

I stroll along a vineyard path,

And there I see the Grapes of Math!

Overhead the sun is blazin',

Soon each grape will be a raisin.

How many grapes are on the vine?

Counting each takes too much time.

Never fear, I have a hunch

There is a match for every bunch!

SNAIL PARADE

One day while walking through a glade,

I came across a snail parade!

Rows and rows of snails I spied,

"How do I count them all?" I cried.

Don't just group the ones you see,

Consider where a snail should be!

ANT ATTACK!

"It's a picnic!" the ants all scream.

How many ants are in this scene?

Try to count them one by one,

Before you finish they'll be done.

Find a square before you count—

Soon you'll see the right amount!

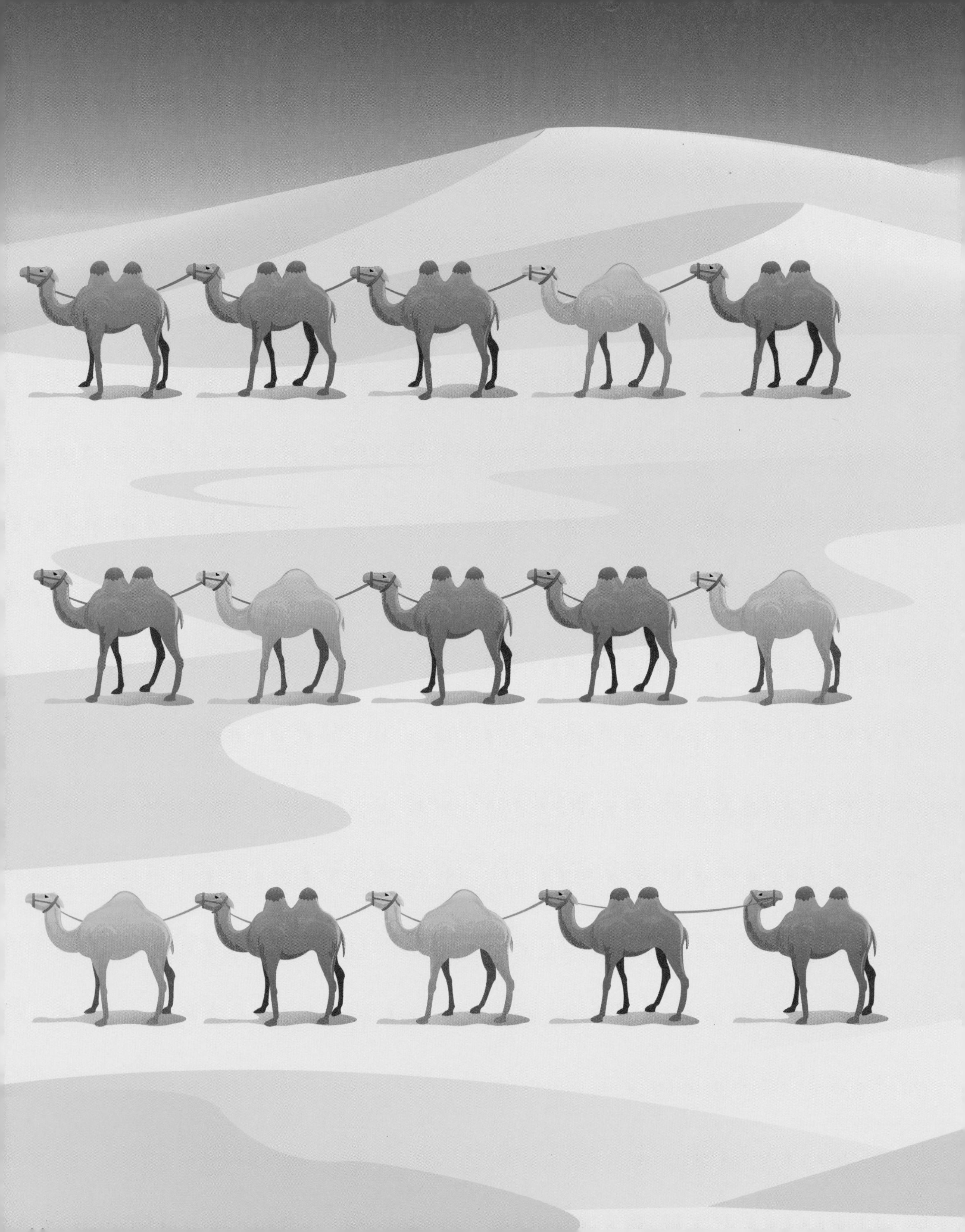

ONE HUMP OR TWO?

Rugged camels on the go,

Their humps are filled with H_2O!

They trek around all day for fun,

Some have two humps, others one.

Can you add the humps you see?

Don't just count them one, two, three . . .

To help you find the right amount,

Group by fives before you count.

SWEET CHERRIES

Apples are crabby, berries are blue,
Cherries are sweet, and so are you!

How many cherries do you see?
Please don't count them separately.

Pair the cherries bunch by bunch,
Add them quick before they're lunch!

DOGGONE IT!

Prairie dogs don't hunt or bark.

They won't protect you in the dark.

Instead they burrow, digging holes,

Making tunnels just like moles!

Can you count the empty mounds?

It's best to just subtract the hounds!

LARGE PIZZA TO GO!

Mama mia, pizza pie,

How many mushrooms do you spy?

Please don't count them, it's too slow,

This hot pie was made to go!

Let me give you some advice,

Just do half and count it twice.

KNOW DICE

Come on, lucky, shiny dice,

Roll a pair and count it twice!

Boxcars, snake eyes, double threes,

Can you add up all of these?

Before you start please look around,

Adding's fast when tens are found.

STRAWBERRY SEEDS

Strawberries grow along the ground.
A better treat cannot be found!

Their seeds reside in tiny rows.
From each of them a plant will grow.

Just how many seeds are there?
Count them only if you dare.

Here's a little trick of mine:
Pair the rows that sum to nine!

WIN-DOZE

I lie in bed and try to sleep,

Counting windows instead of sheep!

How many panes are filled with light?

Here's a way that's really bright.

Don't just count the lights you see.

Subtract the rooms where there's a Zzzzz!

IT'S A BREEZE!

Sometimes when the sun is hot,
A fan is all a lady's got.

The gentle motion of her hand
Brings cool relief that feels just grand.

How many dots adorn this fan?
Add them quickly if you can.

Instead of seeing groups of threes,
Count by fives and it's a breeze!

SCALLOP SURPRISE!

While scallops on the beach look great,

I'd rather see them on my plate.

Unfortunately it's their loss,

They swim their best in butter sauce!

How many scallops in this bunch?

Count them quick, it's time for lunch.

Find a group that does repeat,

Add them up and we can eat!

FLYING SEEDS

When summer days are really hot,

A watermelon hits the spot.

With every messy, juicy bite,

I spit the seeds clear out of sight!

Can you count each little seed?

Here's a hint that you may need.

It's best to pair them slice by slice,

Find a sum, and add it thrice!

IT'S A JUNGLE OUT THERE!

When you're a bug you must beware
Of danger lurking everywhere.

A sticky tongue right on your back,
Soon you're just a tasty snack!

How many beetles do you see?
Count them fast before they flee!

Here's a little helpful fact:
Adding's quick when you subtract!

FOR THE BIRDS

Before you have too big a clan,

It's good to have a housing plan.

Instead of building one big nest,

Lots of small ones may be best!

How many eggs are in this batch?

Count them quick before they hatch.

Here's a hint you can't ignore:

Adding's fast with groups of four!

ANSWERS

FISH SCHOOL

Instead of seeing the fish in rows, look along the diagonal and you will see 4 groups of 4 fish, or 16 fish.

$4 + 4 + 4 + 4 = 16$

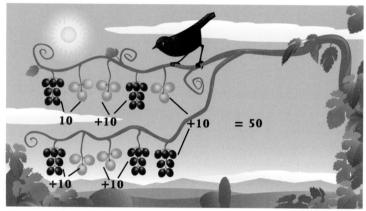

THE GRAPES OF MATH

When possible, add numbers that have easy sums. The grapes can be matched to create 5 pairs which each total 10, so there are 50 grapes altogether.

$10 + 10 + 10 + 10 + 10 = 50$

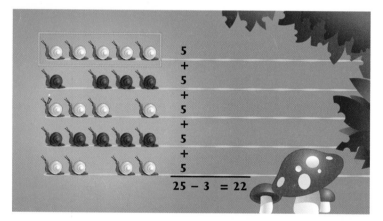

SNAIL PARADE

First imagine 3 snails where they seem to be missing. Then there are 5 rows of 5 snails, or 25 snails. Now subtract the imaginary snails and you are left with 22 snails.

$25 - 3 = 22$

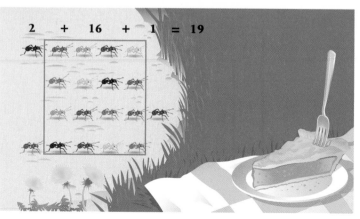

ANT ATTACK!

Find a square consisting of 4 rows of 4 ants, or 16 ants. Add the remaining 3 ants to get 19 ants altogether.

$2 + 16 + 1 = 19$

ONE HUMP OR TWO?

Rather than adding humps across each row, add down along each column. Since each of the 5 columns has 5 humps, there are 25 humps altogether.

$5 + 5 + 5 + 5 + 5 = 25$

SWEET CHERRIES

When possible, add numbers that have easy sums. The cherries can be matched to create 3 pairs which each total 10, so there are 30 cherries altogether.

$10 + 10 + 10 = 30$

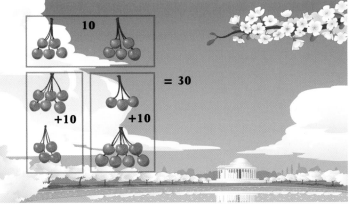

DOGGONE IT!

First count all the mounds by pairing the rows. Each of the 3 pairs has 9 mounds, so there are 27 mounds altogether. Now subtract the 4 prairie dogs and you are left with 23 empty mounds.

$27 - 4 = 23$

LARGE PIZZA TO GO!

Since the pizza is symmetrical, just add up the mushrooms on one half. Double this amount to get 24 mushrooms altogether.

$12 + 12 = 24$

KNOW DICE

Rather than adding pairs of dice, notice that each row has 10 dots. Since there are 4 rows, there are 40 dots altogether.

$10 + 10 + 10 + 10 = 40$

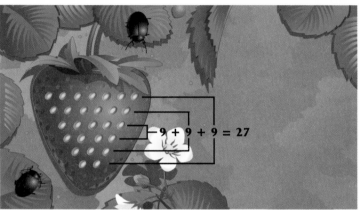

STRAWBERRY SEEDS

Whenever you add consecutive numbers, it is helpful to pair the first and last number, the second and second-to-last number, and so on. All the pairs will have the same total! Here, the 3 pairs each add up to 9, so there are 27 seeds altogether.

$9 + 9 + 9 = 27$

WIN-DOZE

First count all the windows including both the lit and unlit ones. There are 5 windows in each of the 7 columns, or 35 windows altogether. Now subtract the unlit windows and you are left with 28 lit windows.

$35 - 7 = 28$

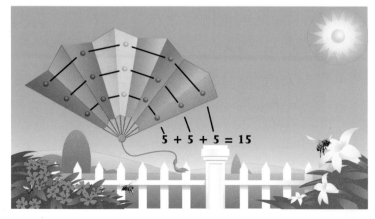

IT'S A BREEZE!

Instead of seeing groups with 3 dots of the same color, look across the fan to see 3 groups each with 5 dots of different colors. There are 15 dots altogether.

$5 + 5 + 5 = 15$

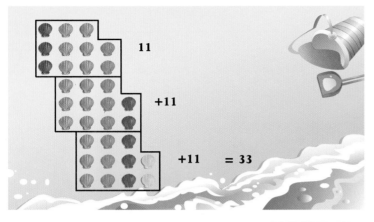

SCALLOP SURPRISE!

Make a group of 11 scallops consisting of those in the top 3 rows. Notice that this pattern repeats itself twice below so there are 33 scallops altogether.

$11 + 11 + 11 = 33$

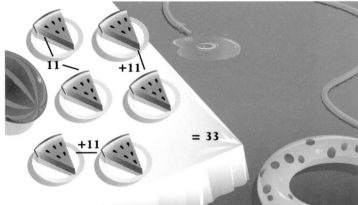

FLYING SEEDS

When possible, add numbers that have easy sums. The slices can be matched to create 3 pairs which each total 11, so there are 33 seeds altogether.

$11 + 11 + 11 = 33$

IT'S A JUNGLE OUT THERE!

First count all 36 creatures by adding along the diagonal. Now subtract the 6 butterflies and inchworms, and you are left with 30 beetles.

$36 - 6 = 30$

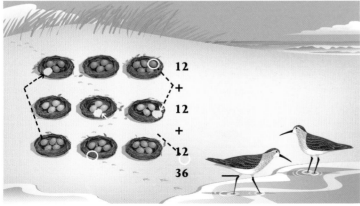

FOR THE BIRDS

If you move one egg from the nests with 5 eggs to those with 3 eggs, then all 9 nests will have 4 eggs. Each row of nests will have 12 eggs, so there are 36 eggs altogether.

$12 + 12 + 12 = 36$

Special thanks to Stephanie Luck,
Daniel Narahara, and Jeffrey Wheeler
for all their creative and artistic help.

ISBN 0-439-59840-0

12 11 10 9 8 7 6 5   5 6 7/0

Printed in the U.S.A.   40
First Bookshelf edition, June 2004

Designed by Marijka Kostiw